Harriet Elizabeth Prescott Spofford

Ballads about Authors

Harriet Elizabeth Prescott Spofford

Ballads about Authors

ISBN/EAN: 9783743308145

Manufactured in Europe, USA, Canada, Australia, Japa

Cover: Foto ©Thomas Meinert / pixelio.de

Manufactured and distributed by brebook publishing software (www.brebook.com)

Harriet Elizabeth Prescott Spofford

Ballads about Authors

HE TROD A MEASURE AS HE WENT,
AND PIPED AND SANG HIS WAY TO FLORENCE.

—*p.* 25

BALLADS

ABOUT AUTHORS

BY
HARRIET PRESCOTT SPOFFORD

ILLUSTRATIONS BY
EDMUND H GARRETT

BOSTON
D LOTHROP COMPANY
FRANKLIN AND HAWLEY STREETS

Copyright, 1887, by D. Lothrop Company.

PRESS OF
Rockwell and Churchill
BOSTON

CONTENTS

Goldsmith's Whistle	13
Samuel Johnson in Uttoxeter Market	29
Blind Milton	49
Beside the Ouse	65
A Splendid Fire	83
Woods of Warwick	99

ILLUSTRATIONS

He trod a measure as he went, And piped and sang his way to Florence.	*Frontis.*
And death confronted him, and awed him	15
Some happy children sat and listened	19
The harp was strung to gentler tune	23
Where the poor bookseller held his stall upon fairing days	33
Even the king sought him proudly	37
Perchance he was doing a penance	41
In silver thunders sobbing slow	48
Tones swelling into gathering tune, Like dark waves swelling to the moon.	51
Ere darkness wrapped the lonely tower	55
The wars of Heaven are fought anew!	59
Cowper and his hares	67
The sunshine seemed a winding-sheet	69

ILLUSTRATIONS.

With lilies floating on its breast	73
In rainbows glowed his garden-side	77
Daydreams once all his own, and hopes	85
Along the streets with heedless haste	89
That night when Collins burned his odes	93
Chaucer's was the verse he carried	101
"Master!" 'twas a cry of music, Queen Titania's voice, oh hearken!	107
"Into lands of antique story, Master, You alone can send us!"	109
Warwick Castle, from the Avon	111

Also portraits and numerous vignettes.

BALLADS
ABOUT AUTHORS

GOLDSMITH'S WHISTLE

GOLDSMITH'S WHISTLE

A LIGHT heart had the Irish lad,
   As light as any in the land,
And surely that was all he had,
   Save the King's English, at command!
Nay, Greek had he, a goodly store,
   Though not a penny came to mock it;
Well, well, and he had something more —
   He had a whistle in his pocket!

Ay, Greek he had, pure root and stem;
   And that they had not at Louvain,
And that they wanted not — for them
   Nor Plato spoke nor Homer sang.
And he had dreamed of classes there,
   And he had crossed the deep seas over,
Determined in a scholar's chair
   With cap and gown to live in clover.

But dean nor don of that famed school
  Cared for the lore the stranger brought,
Greek was not in their time-worn rule,
  And all his silver speech was naught.
Strange land, strange ways, strange faces, too;
  A land that flowed with milk and honey —
And no werd of their tongue he knew,
  And had no stiver of their money.

He supped that night beside the brook,
  That night he slept beneath the hedge;
Dark was the great sky's dreary look,
  Hope gave no promise, fate no pledge.
And when the morning came, despair
  Hung over him, and hunger gnawed him —
He was so young, and life so fair,
  And death confronted him, and awed him.

And then — he was an Irish lad —
  The April in him had its way;
Sun shining, should not one be glad?
  Birds singing, one not match their play?
Soft blew the breeze his tears to wipe,
  And there, upon the grassy hummock,
He laughed at care, and took his pipe,
  And played a tune to stay his stomach.

AND DEATH CONFRONTED HIM, AND AWED HIM.

He played, nor knew of any nigh,
    Lost for the hour in sweet employ,
Till through his dream there stole a cry,
    A little chirping note of joy;
And beating time there, every one,
    With lips that laughed and eyes that glistened,
Like roses burning in the sun
    Some happy children sat and listened.

And scarce less innocent than they
    He gave a nod of merry cheer,
Blew out his cheeks with fresher play,
    And blew the strain out loud and clear.
Clear as the whistling nightingale
    He blew the tuneful moment's fancies,
Sweet airs of ancient Innisfail,
    Or graveside keene, or fleet-foot dances.

And when he ceased, and fain would leave
    The spot, with slower step and slower,
One caught his hand, and one his sleeve,
    And led him to their mother's door.
They brought him honey, brought him bread,
    They swarmed about, a pretty rabble,
And still he heard, when farther sped,
    The music of their unknown babble.

And going on, he knew not where,
  Feet somewhat sore, eyes somewhat dim,
A shadow fell upon the air,
  And suddenly one went with him —
The shadow of remembered song,
  The memory of a mighty singing,
That made the way, late hard and long,
  Light with the music round it ringing;

Carolan's singing, long removed,
  The last of the great bards who blew
Life through old ballads, whom men loved,
  By the same token, whom kings slew.
Still could our wanderer see again
  The streaming beard, the tattered camlet,
The shouldered harp whose throbbing strain
  Brought greeting glad in hall and hamlet.

Not as perchance in elder days,
  When daised ladies bent to hear,
And the torch shed its fitful blaze
  On bull-hide shield and restless spear,
While some old minstrel, gaunt and hoar,
  With "Dathi's Doom" made broadswords rattle,
And the wild song of "Argan Mor"
  Stirred all their hearts to sudden battle;

SOME HAPPY CHILDREN SAT AND LISTENED.

But as beside some cabin door
    The harp was strung to gentler tune,
And hushed the babe the mother bore,
    And hushed the grandam's hapless croon.
While "Usna's Children" called the tear,
    And lovers, moved with tenderer feeling,
Felt all their pulses bound to hear
    "Cushla-ma-chree" and soft "Lough Sheeling."

What music blown on every gale
    Old Carolan was playing then!
What hero's chant, what banshee's wail,
    Our happy wanderer heard again!
The Desmond's love he heard once more
    Sweet Catherine MacCormac gracing,
And saw upon Killarney's shore
    O'Donohue's White Horses racing.

Far off the windy music crept
    To silence; and the startled youth
Laughed at the sudden thought that leapt —
    He was a minstrel, too, forsooth!
Like Carolan, he also went
    To no one but his pipe a debtor,
The earth his bed, the sky his tent —
    A minstrel he, for want of better!

From village green to green his way
    He, too, should pay with pleasant tunes,
While quiet folk, at close of day,
    Broke bread, or in the idle noons.
He, where he saw two lovers lean,
    Could slyly play a "Mina-meala,"
And should a loiterer mischief mean
    Could give the rousing "Fague a ballagh!"

And many a jolly catch complete
    Ballymahon should lend him then;
The "Groves of Blarney," heavenly sweet
    And sad, should melt the hearts of men;
Unwritten song his thoughts o'er-ran,
    From misty time, with stirring story,
Here came the "Humming of the Ban,"
    And here came "Garryone in Glory!"

What bliss, what power, the soul to lead,
    The tear, the smile, a hurrying slave!
Oh, Music, with your rudest reed,
    This one to life and hope you gave!
No more the shady hedge and copse;
    The lad forsook the sheltering byway,
Took out his whistle, tried its stops,
    And bravely trudged along the highway.

THE HARP WAS STRUNG TO GENTLER TUNE.

As fabled beasts before the lyre
   Fell prone, so want and hunger fled;
The way was free to his desire,
   And he like one with manna fed.
The world, the world, for him was meant,
   Cathedral towers, and Alpine torrents!
He trod a measure as he went,
   And piped and sang his way to Florence!

Great wit and scholar though he be,
   I love, of all his famous days,
This time of simple vagrancy
   Ere youth and bliss had parted ways.
With what a careless heart he strayed,
   Light as the down upon a thistle,
Made other hearts his own, and paid
   His way through Europe with a whistle!

SAMUEL JOHNSON
IN UTTOXETER MARKET

Samuel Johnson in Uttoxeter Market

STORIES there are in the world which make the heart ache with their sadness,
Stories of war and of want, stories of horror and death,
Parting of lovers forever, wrongs ending only in madness,
Mourning of mothers for those who scarce knew the sweetness of breath.

Not such a story as any of these is the tale I shall tell you,
Through chains or conspiracies here nobody suffers or dies,
Simple it is, my child, as anything ever befell you,
And yet when I chance to recall it I find there are tears in my eyes

Ah, there are chains full as strong as dungeon
    chains binding the prisoner,
But none hear them clank when remorse comes to
    murder the peace,
Nor torture is worse than the still small voice that
    makes you a listener,
That seldom in all a long life gave the one that I
    speak of release.

Strong was the sun in Uttoxeter Market and sharp
    were the showers there,
Where the poor bookseller held his stall upon fair-
    ing days;
Making his two-penny bargains many and long
    were the hours there
Spent by the debt-ridden man, worn with the world
    and its ways.

Books of the day were about him, and books that
    were ancient and far-fet,
All a good company, golden and silvern their words,
Yet hushed were their voices when fair-day came
    in Uttoxeter Market,
Stilled by the bleating of calves and the lowing of
    herds.

What would the good-wife with warble of Shakespeare or speech of Sylvester,
Bouncing about on her pillion, with butter and
  eggs on her lap —
Better her pocket-piece tossed to the tumbling
  clown or the jester,
She with an eye to a ribbon, she to a grogram,
  mayhap!

What would the yeoman with blackletter folio, or
  pages of Latin,
Tales of Venetian adventurers, troublous to spell —
He had his filly to brag of, shining and sleeker
  than satin,
He had his little black pigs and his yearlings to
  sell!

Hard was the task then, believe me, to earn the
  poor shilling so needed,
Sore ached the old bookseller's back, and sore
  ached his pride,
Yet often and often he thought how lightly the
  time would have speeded
if he could only have had there his son by his
  side.

Dear was the boy to his heart, dearer perhaps that
 disaster
Had scarred his sad face with the evil that good
 Queen Anne's touch had not stayed —
Was there a work on his shelves of which the boy
 was not yet master?
Was there a lad in all Litchfield not by his book-
 lore dismayed?

Oft the old father turned over some scheme that
 should send him to college,
Surely with barely a crust were he and the mother
 content,
Bitter the trial to think they must starve this
 yearning for knowledge
While gold all over the kingdom for frivolous
 pleasure was spent.

Strong was the sun on that day when all of his
 ails so oppressed him,
Long and laborious the walk, and heavy his heart
 with his care —
Could the boy go in his place, for once, how kindly
 'twould rest him,
Could he but linger, for once, at home in his easy-
 chair!

WHERE THE POOR BOOKSELLER HELD HIS STALL UPON FAIRING DAYS.

Did the boy hear him aright? He go to Uttoxeter
  Market?
He with his tremors and scars, he with his beg-
  garly clothes,
He with his purblind eyes, for every wit's sally a
  target,
He to hawk ballads for ribalds and boors with
  their laughter and oaths?

Betimes, were there not at the door every morning three lads out of many,
One bowing the back to receive him, the others
  supporting his state?
Was he not first in the classes? Did they com-
  pare him with any?
He, who had writ Greek pentameters to stand in
  a stall and to wait?

Yet oft on the long-withdrawn highway the sight
  of a tired old man walking,
As sunshine and sunshower succeeded, that morning swam o'er the boy's eyes,
With the call of the doves overhead came the sound
  of a voice that was hawking
Wares that few wanted, a weary old voice that
  was quavering with sighs.

That was the morning when, climbing for apples,
    he came across Petrarch,
And nothing to him was the world then for hour
    after hour,
Nothing was bookworm or beggar, nothing was
    Cæsar or Tetrarch,
He in Italian gardens lost like a bee in a flower!

But seeing again the white face, out of which life
    and courage were sinking,
Did his heart smite him to meet there the tender
    reproach of that gaze?
When at nightfall, all sore and disheartened, the
    father sat dreaming and thinking,
Did there not cross the boy's fancy the difference
    between their two days?

One in the heat and the hurry of barter, the cry-
    ing and calling,
Dizzy and dazed with the noise, longing for twi-
    light's relief —
One in green coolness and shadow, with murmur-
    ous waters soft falling,
And sweet was the melody round him, and sweet
    was the myrtle's crushed leaf!

EVEN THE KING SOUGHT HIM PROUDLY.

All at once such a warmth of affection, such flood
 of regretting,
Rushed to the heart of the boy, with such fervor
 of pity and grief —
Ah, if he only had spoken it, then had been space
 for forgetting,
Nor of sorrows to haunt a whole lifetime had that
 been the chief!

"Unfilial, undutiful child," his words went repeating, repeating,
And still, as the tone of the gong in the isles of
 the orient wrought,
Touched with the tap of a finger, rolls mightily
 swelling and beating
Till it fills the whole sky with its sound, were
 those words in his thought.

Still did they sigh in his thought, when the father
 had sought his long slumber,
And he in his nest of singing-birds, in the old
 university town,
Filled night with revel and madcap pranks, or days
 without number
Bathed in Castalian waters, and gathered the bays
 for his crown.

Still they resounded about him, in all the ripe years, with their grieving,
Hid in his work, while the murmur of fame babbled on like a brook,
Work that grew glorious what time the evergreen chaplet was weaving —
Ah, what a fragrance those bays have to-day, though pressed in a book!

Umpire of scholars at last, and heir of all learning owned loudly,
Poets, and painters, and players, confessed to his mastery each,
Princes and statesmen inquired of him, even the king sought him proudly —
He the king of the people, and he the king of their speech!

But still through his plaudits resounded the words once so long ago uttered,
"Unfilial, undutiful child," till no more could he bear his own sighs,
And whenever the leaves of his book he dreamily fingered and fluttered
Swam there the white old face with the tender reproach of its eyes.

PERCHANCE HE WAS DOING A PENANCE.

Sharp fell the showers then, one fair-day, across
    the Uttoxeter Market,
And, jostled and hustled and chided, another old
    man trod its ways;
Eager the crowd and the cries as of yore, while
    he stood there the target
For every wit's sally, the magnet for every lout's
    gaze.

Where once was the bookseller's stall, stood the
    burly old fellow,
Purblind, unwieldy, bare-headed in all of the rain,
Sharing the gape of the rustics with smart Punchi-
    nello,
Half like a Caliban, half like a demigod writhing
    in pain.

Naught of the flout and the fleer did he know, or
    the jibes that were spoken,
Old memories, old forms thronged about him, there
    in the market-place,
Old voices fell sweet on his ear till his heart was
    half broken,
Prayers parted his lips, I think, and tears poured
    down over his face.

Perchance he was doing a penance with strange superstition,
Erst he refused the deed in the strength of his selfish shame,
Now, fifty long years and more gone, in impassioned contrition,
Known the world over, he stood there, and humbled his pride and his fame.

Let wild Hebrew chief or Greek King offer up his heart's treasure —
Better than sacrifice, once said the prophet, it is to obey —
Yet costly as any, the name and the glory, I measure,
Offered up on the shrine of Uttoxeter Market that day!

BLIND MILTON

IN SILVER THUNDERS SOBBING SLOW.

BLIND MILTON

Dark were the shadows of the room
As Valombrosa's green-arched gloom;
Only the organ-pipes' dim row
Sent through the dusk a golden glow,
As yearning for the Master's hand
Their slumbering secrets to command
And pour wild music out, until
Deep melancholy's sweetest will
Had utterance, luxurious woe
In silver thunders sobbing slow.

For his was all the subtle art
Of melody that breaks the heart
With rapture. And delicious shocks,
Sweet as the honey of the rocks
To other sense, well did he know
From dulcet stops to breathe and blow —

Tones swelling into gathering tune,
Like dark waves swelling to the moon,
While the rapt soul sank whelmed and drowned,
Lost in the tumult of vast sound!

And all that larger music, too,
The music of our speech, he knew;
Word meeting word in melting rhyme
As birds sing in the dewy prime,
Fleet syllables to ordered ways
Moving in pomp of ringing phrase
And haunting memory with their line,
Like mighty clarions clear and fine
On mountain echoes lingering long —
Great Milton, Master of all song!

Now in the gloom the Master sate,
Blind, silent, old, and desolate.
Yet full the light about the pole
And firmament of his high soul!
And there great forms around him came,
He heard sweet voices call his name,
He fought old fights and, bearding fate,
Splendid and perfect shaped the State.
Still his blood burns, his chamber rings,
As when he bandied words with kings!

TONES SWELLING INTO GATHERING TUNE,
LIKE DARK WAVES SWELLING TO THE MOON.

There, too, came pictures of the days,
With free feet set in fortunate ways,
When, winged with youth and poesy,
The under heaven of Italy
Was his — just after that glad prime
When Comus led his sylvan mime,
And, as some spring in sunshine slips,
"L'Allegro" bubbled from his lips —
And his did hoar horizons bend
With Galileo for his friend!

But yesternight, it seemed, that hour
He climbed to find the lonely tower
Of Arcetri, where the sad sage
Sat like some older archimage
'Midst his black arts, who weighed the sun,
Saw hidden moons their courses run,
Watched the earth spin, and wrought his spell
Even from the Inquisition's cell,
And, while the door slid in its grooves,
Cried to himself, "And still it moves!"

Had Galileo seen the youth
Climbing the hill, the rose, in sooth,
Bright on his cheek as on a girl's,
Along his shoulder yellow curls,

And lithe and strong his limbs, his tread
Like one who walks on air instead
Of common earth, he might have thought
Some young Greek god his wand had brought —
Had the remorseless heavens spared
Sight to the eyes their depths had bared!

Yet could but his old heart rejoice
At the fresh sweetness of that voice,
And with high converse fill the hour
Ere darkness wrapped the lonely tower.
Ah! what a night, my Milton, then
Opened the deep skies to thy ken,
When Galileo raised his glass
And bade the great procession pass,
With spirits quickening from their cars,
With dancing of the dædal stars!

There belted planets, horned moons,
Swam as to rhythm of unheard tunes;
There, circling in far frosty lines,
Old Mazzaroth led out his signs;
And as his race some lampad runs
Ran red Arcturus with his sons.

"Its darkness wrapped the lonely tower"

Where this white host their lustre trailed
Were these the Pleiades unveiled?
Whose was this sword-flame cleft the sky?
And was that Ashtoreth went by?

Ah, what strange joys that fateful hour
Brought to him on the lonely tower!
What wild throbs called his soul to arms
With starry challenge like alarms
From silver trumpets, while his sense
Swooned in eclipse, and power immense
Swept up with him and turned the keys
Upon undreamed eternities!
What depths he pierced, what glories trod,
Till the last glory showed him God!

Alas, alas, how fallen here
These long years later! Sphere o'er sphere
So that Great Spirit fell before
From heights of heaven. Now heaven no more
For him who, darkling, blind, and old,
Sees morning's rose nor evening's gold,
The smile of children sees, nor eyes
Tender as stars in twilight skies.
Sovereigns dishonor, friends disown,
Blind, in the dark, he sits alone.

Alone? Who throng the portals then,
Companions towering more than men?
Into what amplitude of space
Open the walls of that sad place?
What courts where, white as ancient frost,
Stand seraphs, with their wide wings crossed,
Where shining captains come and go,
Where tides of battle ebb and flow,
And where, as in the farthest blue,
The wars of heaven are fought anew!

Alone, when from the outer towers
Lean Dominations, Virtues, Powers?
When, in wan splendor Lucifer
Pauses till all the pulses stir,
With Uriel, of the Seven that one
Whom John saw standing in the sun?
And blind, who with undazzled sight
Meets the inviolate source of light,
And, while archangels keep the posts,
Sees face to face the Lord of Hosts?

Oh, Milton, singing thy great hymn
And quiring with the cherubim,
Thou art not blind, or sad, or old,
Thou hast no part in dark grave-mould,

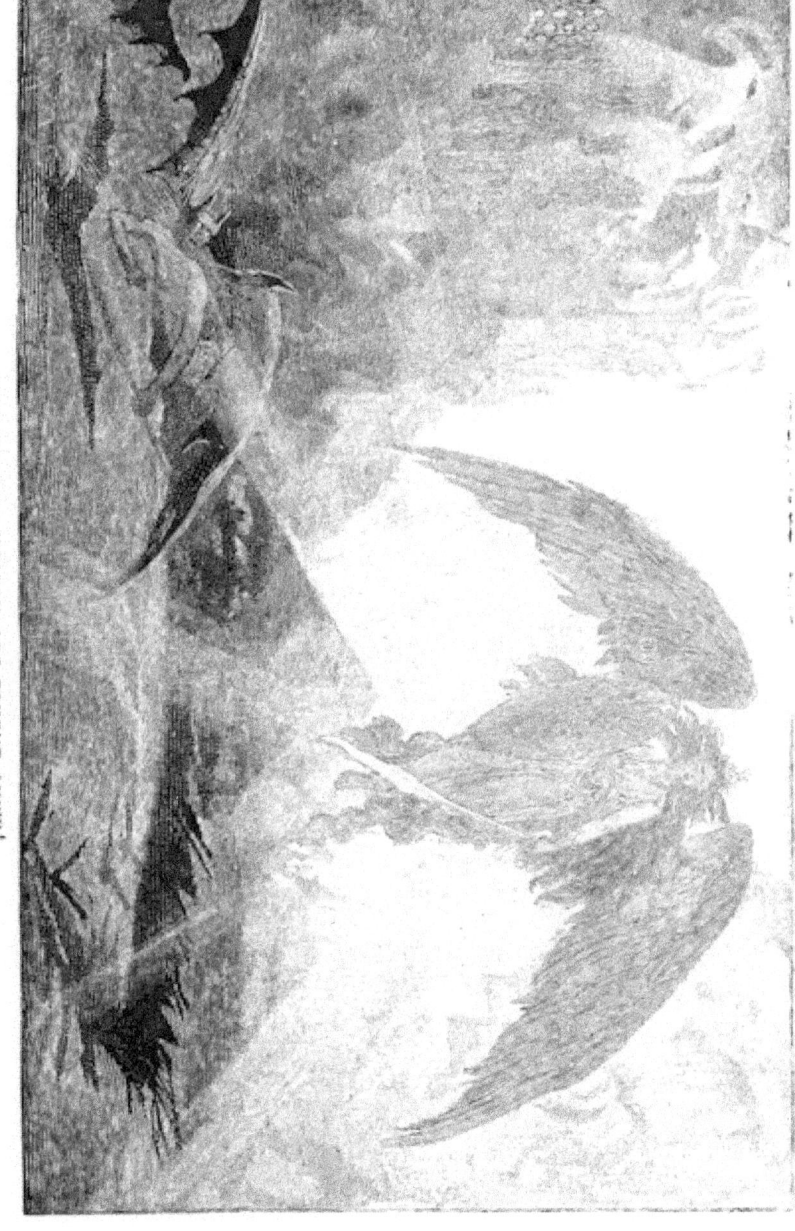

THE WARS OF HEAVEN ARE FOUGHT ANEW!

Forever fair and blithe and young
And deathless as thy golden tongue!
The nightingale upon thy bough
Sang never half so sweet as thou,
And could'st thou only sing to me
I would be blind that thou might'st see!

BESIDE THE OUSE

How often, in my childish days,
    Pausing amid her many cares,
My mother used to tell to me
    The simple tale of Cowper's hares.

The slender history never tired,
    Each pretty puss seemed half my own.
And real as the sounds I knew
    Their sad and kindly playmate's tone.

And, later, with the lines he wrote
    His mother, in as hearty grief,
The tears poured down my little face
    To run with his along the leaf.

And so, you see, I always loved
   The gentle poet; and if word,
Ever so idle, went abroad
   Concerning Cowper, that I heard.

Thus, it may be, this story came;
   And if the whole be hardly true,
Yet one so like it surely chanced
   That, as I heard, I tell it you.

Sweet clouded soul! But as the pearl
   In heaven's great gate, whose clouded light
Was heaven's own lustre filtering through—
   A soul was never made more white!

And yet he thought that soul was dark
   With foul desires, and soiled with sin,
And when he swept and garnished it
   There seven devils entered in.

And far in black eternities,
   While wild cold tremors o'er him ran,
He saw himself engulfed and lost,
   Lost to the love of God or man!

He who loved God with childish faith,
  Who loved his fellow-man with joy,
Who passed his long quiescent days
  In every innocent employ!

COWPER AND HIS HARES.

But still the blur upon the brain
  Compelled him with the monstrous boast:
His the unpardonable sin,
  The sin against the Holy Ghost!

Friends might be pitying, tender tears
  Dear Mary Unwin's eyes might dim —
They, first of all, the vile truth known,
  Anathemas must hurl at him!

Malignant blur! It wrapped the world
  At morning. And when night was deep
He shuddered, by a flaming sword
  Shut from the paradise of sleep.

He walked his garden, turned his books,
  In an impenetrable gloom;
The sunshine seemed a winding-sheet,
  A child's light laugh a sound of doom.

And could there gladness be with those
  Of death and foul decay the slaves?
They who were happy only danced
  Where roses masked the yawning graves!

Naught in the world he saw but death,
  And after death — ah, what fell curse
Had withered love in that dark power,
  The power that ruled the universe!

THE SUNSHINE SEEMED A WINDING-SHEET.

As when the moon swims large and low
   O'er level lands, and up her height
Come creeping vapors from the marsh
   To veil her melancholy light —

Then slowly steals a greater gloom,
   Earth's mightier shadow sweeping there,
Till swoons the orb in blind eclipse —
   So his dejection was despair.

Despair! And wherefore live to feel
   Its pangs, when everlasting sleep
Hung but one moment's reach away —
   That sleep so cold, so white, so deep!

No, no, he would not longer bear
   This loathsome agony of fear!
The horrors of the vast unknown —
   Those horrors were about him here!

Where softly flowed the river Ouse
   Through dell and dingle sparkling chill,
With willows whitening to the wind,
   The pools were deep, the pools were still.

In some dark pool were place for him,
    Were peace, profoundest peace, at last,
Were rest beneath the placid flow —
    His rest, before the night were past!

With eager haste he hailed his man,
    Mounted beside him in the chaise;
Nerved as the bow-string to the shaft
    That night he went his devious ways.

A mile or two of lonely lane,
    A turning, and the river crept
Glimmering beside the path he knew,
    And on its breast the lilies slept.

The night was dark, the wind was up
    Chasing the stars with cloud on cloud,
Now stripped a great sky bare, and now
    Hung all the heavens in a shroud.

But he nor fleece of stars nor cloud
    Beheld, nor heard the shrill wind blow;
Forces of night and evil, he
    Defied them, stupefied with woe.

WITH LILIES FLOATING ON ITS BREAST.

He did not heed the fragrant way
  Where wanton bramble-roses grew,
Now where great flowering branches stretched
  And brushed his face with showers of dew.

And when from sheltered nightingales
  Far off the bubbling flute-note stole
On long swells of the wind, he heard
  Only the cry of some lost soul.

Naught of the wonted way he marked;
  He saw no turning of the lane,
Nor constellations wheeling high —
  Lost in his revery of pain.

He only saw the dusky pool
  With lilies floating on its breast,
Where stars flashed, too, with breaking rays,
  Where all things bade to dreamless rest.

How slumberously above would move
  Those waters dallying on their way;
How cool the quiet depths should be
  After this torrid fever's sway!

The old horse kept his moping pace,
    The man beside him dozed once more;
He had not thought the way so far —
    Had the lane left the river-shore?

Again in moody musings plunged,
    He noted not the winding road
Far from the reedy river-bed
    Where Ouse among his rushes flowed.

The wind went down; from distant farms
    The cocks crowed with their rousing cheer;
A silver ether swathed the east
    Where one great star hung like a tear.

A bird half warbled in his sleep,
    Another answered him and woke,
And all the leafy countryside
    To clangor of wild music broke;

And odors met him full of balm;
    Pallid he saw the fainting blue,
Peace in the sky of rosy gold —
    And in his heart what strange peace, too!

IN RAINBOWS GLOWED HIS GARDEN-SIDE.

For as the way through hedgerows wound,
    The way familiar grown of late,
In rainbows glowed his garden-side,
    The old horse paused before his gate!

All night, in vain, he sought the pool
    Where still the glimmering river flowed,
All night in vain pursued his end,
    Purblind along the circling road.

All night he sought with sense absorbed
    His solemn tryst with death to keep,
All night some power withstood — that power
    Which holds the planets where they sweep!

Was it, indeed, that mighty power
    Which sways the stars and feeds the sun,
That led this poor bewildered man
    Ere he was utterly undone?

He thought so. And he gathered hope,
    And life's pale flame streamed up anew.
If other power — I cannot name
    Its sweet puissance. Pray can you?

A SPLENDID FIRE

SPLENDID FIRE
WILLIAM COLLINS

How dim, how drear, these narrow streets,
   These London streets before the dawn!
What solitude the stroller meets,
   What sense of human life withdrawn!

Down alleys where the darkness gropes
   What mad and mocking phantoms lurk —
Phantoms of daydreams and of hopes
   Fled to thin air and lost in murk!

Daydreams once all his own, and hopes
   That, fluttering gay with frolic sports,
Led him a witch-dance up the slopes
   Beyond his quiet college courts;

Up to the town with all its sway,
    Its stir of letters and of art,
Players, and playhouse, and the play
    Where he should bear his tragic part —

Through midnight streets, as now, should bear,
    Forlorn and fierce, his tragic part,
No bright hopes beckoning, but despair
    Laying a chill hand on his heart.

Fair Magdalen tower, bright Oxford spires,
    In fancy fading on the view,
How softly fall your topmost fires
    As down these streets he looks at you!

How kindly seems, this lonesome night,
    The shelter that you used to give
While in your walls he longed for flight,
    And longed a larger life to live.

And he the larger life full soon
    Has lived, and all its joys has learned,
Has touched an antique lyre to tune —
    And song and singer have been spurned.

DAYDREAMS ONCE ALL HIS OWN, AND HOPES. . . . .

A SPLENDID FIRE.

For, all the passionate strain he sung,
   The lyric line, the echoing ode,
Upon insensate ears has rung,
   And round unanswering hearts has flowed.

Forth for the plaudit all a-flush
   His whole soul leaned — and not a cry
Gave him acclaim. Into that hush
   What should he do but sink and die!

That awful hush, where dreams, inspired,
   A chord of voices heard instead,
Voices of those his soul desired
   As starving children long for bread.

And, fair illusive folly, too,
   Fame spread her wings of rainbowed gauze —
Now silence where her trumpet blew,
   And darkness where her dazzle was.

An instrument of sweetest sound
   Where all Æolian murmurs swim,
Tune under tune in subtlest round —
   How had the world entreated him!

A sacred anger beads his brow,
    And of a sudden stays his breath;
Since all the world rejects them, now
    His songs shall have a glorious death!

Along the streets with heedless haste
    He strides to find his dingy room,
No more the midnight oil to waste —
    A greater flame shall light its gloom!

With trembling hands he tears the leaves
    And scatters them about the hearth;
A wasting sob his bosom heaves,
    He laughs with half-demoniac mirth.

There lie they, darlings of his life,
    His life of six-and-twenty years;
In them what swift triumphant strife,
    In them what thrills and joyous tears!

This line — the day it came, a flood
    Of rosy light o'erflowed his brain;
And that — so swelled the bubbling blood
    His heart ached with delicious pain.

Sheet after sheet, and leaf on leaf —
    The night is cold, the night is dark,
The night consorts with such a grief;
    Now haste, and fetch the kindling spark!

Ah, what a billowy flame is that
    Leaps up the chimney in its flight,
Was ever fire such lustre gat
    To squander on the outer night!

What colors flash along the blaze
    That spreads its wings, and soars and dips!
So burns, long soaked in salty sprays,
    Driftwood of wrecked and stranded ships.

Now curls the precious manuscript
    Of Music on the Grecian Stage,
And none the sweetness that it dripped
    Shall know, to the remotest age.

What light it casts about the place!
    How paints upon the eager eye
The festal throng, the sandy space,
    The sounding sea, the azure sky!

While monstrous shadows steal in groups —
   Medea's dagger in her eyes,
Electra, broken-hearted, droops,
   Orestes from his Furies flies.

It shrivels in a blackening scroll;
   Gone those great shadows half divine,
But still on the reluctant coal
   The swarming sparks re-write the line.

Another to the fire he flings;
   He listens, and his face is wan —
For him, as for the Spanish Kings,
   Tolls the great Bell of Arragon!

At last, at last, let glory burst
   From one sole page athwart the gloom
That drinks it as a thing athirst
   And blossoms into morning bloom!

While all the thronging "Passions" troop,
   As once before they hurrying came,
And for a flashing moment stoop
   Emblazoned on the ruddy flame:

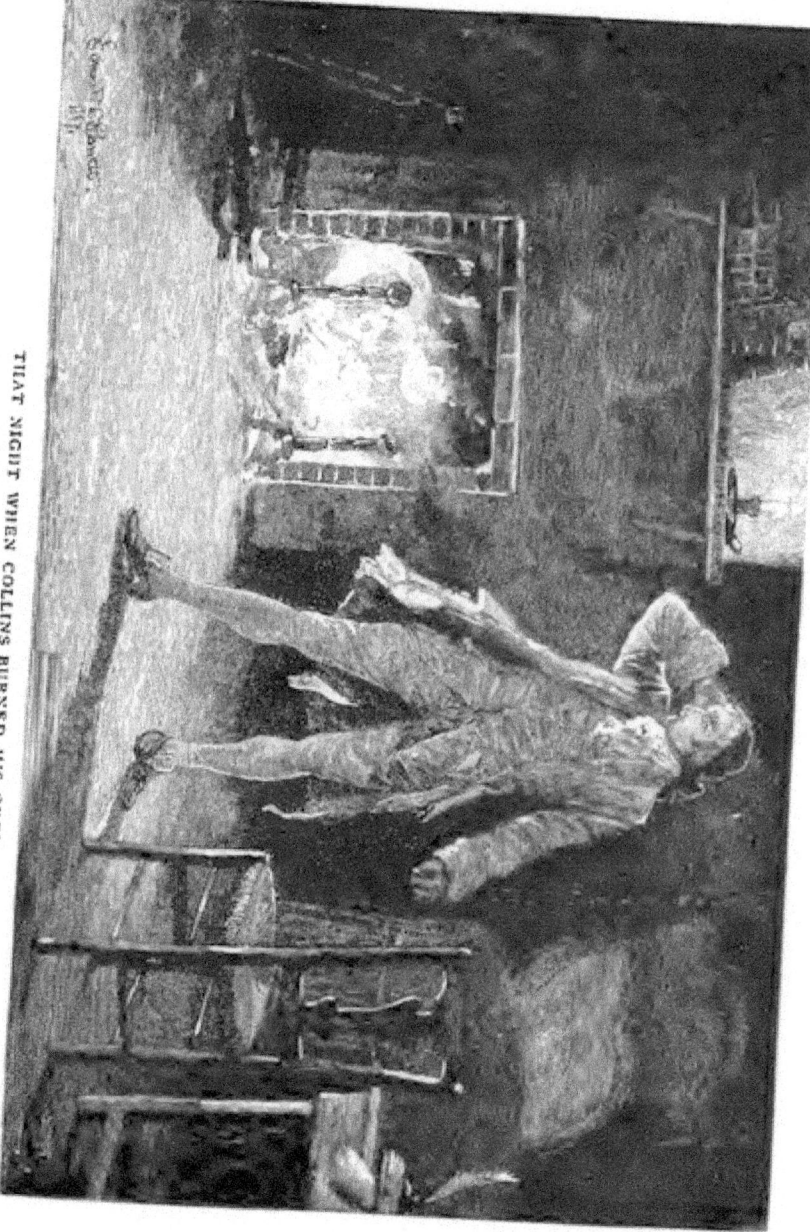

THAT NIGHT WHEN COLLINS BURNED HIS ODES.

Pale Melancholy, paler Fear,
  And Anger with his secret stings,
Sport brandishing his beechen spear,
  Love shaking odors from his wings.

They pass; they fade; his life fades, too,
  Hope waves no more her golden hair;
One only of the wondrous crew
  Lingers, in ashes — 'tis Despair.

But splendid was the fire that roared,
  And full the woes and wild distress
About it in libation poured,
  Lees of the wine of bitterness!

Surely no altar ever raised
  The smoke of sacrificial loads
With loftier, sadder fires than blazed
  That night when Collins burned his odes!

WOODS OF WARWICK

WOODS OF WARWICK.

PLEASANT, pleasant woods of Warwick, when the
    shaws are thick with summer:
Green and golden, gloom and sunshine, leafy wealth
    of wilderness;
Velvet mosses plashing rainbows round the feet of
    any comer
Lingering where the dew still lingers, branches
    droop, and odors press;
High above the castle towers; down below the wild
    brook brawling;
And across a dream of sorrow, hark! the nightin-
    gales are calling
Far away in long-drawn depths of dusky dell and
    dark recess.

I was never there, were you, dear? Yet at once, my eyelids closing,
Thrice a hundred years have vanished and a tender hand I lay
On this ancient tree-bole's furrows, crooked gnarls and knots, supposing
When 'twas young a lad I know of chanced to stroll this self-same way;
Warbling wood-notes as he loitered, and, the blood in blushes bringing —
While a cuckoo mocked, and madly many thrushes burst out singing —
Here Will Shakespeare, it may happen, cut the name "Anne Hatheway!"

Thrush, or cuckoo? Nay, beshrew me! did he see that cuckoo mocking
When he turned his head to listen and his fancy felt the spell?
In his hand — its sweetest secrets under old black-letter locking —
Chaucer's was the verse he carried, opening where the pages tell
Of the elf-queen and her people when the land was full of fairy.

CHAUCER'S WAS THE VERSE HE CARRIED . . . .

Thrush, or cuckoo? Nay, a gladsome spirit, delicate and airy,
Nay, an airy spirit was it of the name of Ariel!

On the turf he threw him gaily with old Chaucer for his pillow;
Far along the level greenwood where he sent a happy eye
Wind and boughs and latest sunbeams swept in billow over billow,
Oxlips and the nodding violets danced between him and the sky,

Wild thyme and the sweet musk-roses sent their
    fragrance out to find him,
There a jewelled snake slipped leaving his enamelled
    skin behind him,
Bees with brimming honey-bags, and big and burly,
    blundered by.

Was he sure it was a snake then wore the gilded
    weed and cleft it?
"Weed," he murmured, "wide enough to wrap a
    fairy in." And might
That Titania be, who doffed the gauzy coverlid and
    left it,
Hovering in the gentle gloom, and shining there in
    sheer delight?
Was the bee that just sung by him, where the shade
    was deep and mellow,
Kind Hobgoblin, loved of firesides, he the shrewd
    and knavish fellow,
Was that Puck, the lob of spirits, merry wanderer
    of the night?

Evening sun forsook the forest, twilight gathered in
    the hollows;
Winds went rustling, dewy coolness fell like shadow
    on the air;
Where the new moon hung, the leaves stirred like
    the wings of darting swallows;
Where the new moon, slight and glorious, hung a
    sudden silver flare,
In its lovely crescent swiftly stole a glimmering
    apparition,
Lost among the tossing branches, half a dream and
    half a vision,
Oberon, the king of fairies, in that moment passing
    there!

Hist! No whisper! In the royal lustre who were
    these came trooping?
What gay swarm of silken banners, wings, and
    scarfs of damask dyes?
Topsy-turvy, hurly-burly, tripping, tumbling, soaring,
    swooping,
All the elves in humming murmur of light laughs
    and rippling cries!

Cobweb, floating through the darkness, filmy as a
    bat and slender;
Balancing above a poppy, Moth with wings of downy
    splendor;
And Peasblossom, flower or fairy, fluttering with the
    butterflies!

"Master!" 'Twas a cry of music, Queen Titania's
    voice, oh hearken!
"Though, indeed, you know the summer still doth
    tend upon my state—"
Breathe not, think not! She all rosy glows while
    shadows round her darken!
"Yet I fain of other lands would tempt the pleas-
    ures, try the fate.
Running stream no fairy ventures, witch nor war-
    lock crosses water,
Woe betide the sorry elf if urchins of the great
    seas caught her!
Yet, beyond them, richer roses, sweeter nightingales
    must wait."

"MASTER!" 'TWAS A CRY OF MUSIC, QUEEN TITANIA'S VOICE, OH HEARKEN!

"INTO LANDS OF ANTIQUE STORY, MASTER, YOU ALONE
CAN SEND US."

Have you, with a south-wind blowing, heard a harp-
 string's silver shiver?
Oberon, the king, was speaking: "Fairy-land obeys
 my nod,

And, though like a forester I these groves may
    tread forever,
Let me break a lance, I pray you, with some
    chapleted Greek god!
Into lands of antique story, Master, you alone can
    send us,
One midsummer night's mad revel in Athenian
    forests lend us!
We are Gothic fairies, take us where the fauns of
    Greece have trod!"

"Master, Master," chimed the chorus, "we are
    homebred English fairies,
We the little people who, the old dame tells you,
    bless the hearth,
Sweep the dust behind the door, and churn the
    cream in lucky dairies,
Dance within the nine-men's-morris, haunt the
    nightside with our mirth,
Light us tapers from the waxen thighs of humble-
    bees, and cheery
Blow our elfin horns and scatter when the stars do.
    But we weary,
Long for other sports, and weary of this corner of
    the earth!"

Night came sweeping through the forest, soft her
   sombre garments trailing;
With a sound of gallant chiding distant hounds
   began to bay;
Like a shoal of dancing waters in the moon, the
   crew went sailing,
Like a cloud of flying rose-leaves when the winds
   are up and away.
"Following darkness like a dream," sighed Will
   Shakespeare half in sadness,
Underneath his breath, and spelled in this mid-
   summer night's dream madness,
All the woods of Warwick ringing with the elfin
   roundelay.

WARWICK CASTLE, FROM THE AVON.

www.ingramcontent.com/pod-product-compliance
Lightning Source LLC
Chambersburg PA
CBHW031407160426
43196CB00007B/934